he'll

~~nathan dueck~~

to kelly, victoria, & beckett.
from uncle farmer sausage.
(the original porker)

nathSweek

Pedlar Press | St John's

COPYRIGHT © 2014 nathan dueck

ALL RIGHTS RESERVED. No part of this book may be reproduced or transmitted in any form or by any means whatsoever without written permission from the publisher, except by a reviewer, who may quote brief passages in a review. For information, write Pedlar Press at 113 Bond Street, St John's NL A1C 1T6 Canada.

ACKNOWLEDGEMENTS
The publisher wishes to thank the Canada Council for the Arts and the NL Publishers Assistance Program for their generous support of our publishing program.

LIBRARY AND ARCHIVES CANADA CATALOGUING IN PUBLICATION

Dueck, Nathan, 1979-, author
    He'll [sic] / Nathan Dueck.

Poems.
ISBN 978-1-897141-62-5 (pbk.)

    1. Title.

PS8557.U28145H4 2014   C811'.6
C2014-900061-8

COVER ART Mark Peckmezian

DESIGN Zab Design & Typography

Printed in Canada

ACKNOWLEDGEMENTS

my gratitude to editor Jeramy Dodds for taking the time, to publisher Beth Follett for taking it on, to designer Zab for taking it all in.

gratitude to the editors who published some of these poems in earlier versions: "Our Husband" in *Canadian Literature*; "The Teetotaler's Rhapsody" in *Contemporary Verse 2*; "Article of Faith" & "Proberb" in *Rampike*; "Notes" & "*Gesangbuch der Mennoniten* / Transposition" in *Rhubarb*.

to my parents, my siblings, and friends who make up my family. to Hans Werner for correcting my *Plaut'dietsch*. & to Oana Avasilichioaei, Di Brandt, Lori Emerson, Jon Paul Fiorentino, David Foster, Robert Kroetsch, Patrick Friesen, Owen Percy, Robyn Read, Mark Sampson, Aritha van Herk, & Rachel Zolf for reading drafts.

for Sharon, who understands.

he'll

A NOTE ON THE TEXT

    I WAS RAISED INDOORS BY PARENTS ATTEMPTING TO SPARE ME from developing allergies or asthma. Mother indulged my bookish inclinations, borrowing a shelf's worth of hymnals in noble German alongside sheaves of humble English novels. Father assigned me a related duty: I was to translate sheets of *Hüag'dietsch* and *Enjelsch* lines into *Plaut'dietsch*, our mother tongue,[1] a plain-spoken parlance with the cadence, intonation, and tempo of the Canadian prairies. Such a learned chore was common in Mennonite — *ooda Mennoniet* — households like mine, for we were formally illiterate, in spite of our fluency with a peculiar Germanic vernacular, yet in the first half of the twentieth century a daughter normally assumed that responsibility.

    I weighed those emasculating experiences against the task of translating the work in your hands. I unearthed a store of *Hüag'dietsch* and *Plaut'dietsch* sources, or *ur*-texts, "The Heel He Hurt While Fleeing Hell Will Heal In Time," from a manila envelope lodged behind the card catalogue, beneath crates of microfiche, near the stacks of the East Village Public Library. The manuscript, after a manner of speaking, was mailed to "Mrs. Shepard Harold Hamm" from "R. Dyck," without a return address, and post-marked Rat River, Manitoba, 1979. The document from which this ersatz version is bowdlerized, was made up of ornate "poesy" typed onto 8½" x 11" corrasable bond. Judging by the amount of murine excreta in that irascible package, a nest of rodents rummaged through its contents, ravaging edges. Please place this earthy "œuvre," O reader, in any order you will.

    While you pore over these translations, note the tensions between languages you hear, read, and speak. As you while away time to get ahold of the present babble, notice how this fervid pedant, like its unknown author, grasps at the

---

1. I maintain a respect for *onsa Mutta'sproak* as a means of communication. Its true capacity to express humour has been amply explored elsewhere. Unfortunately, other texts tend to sustain the mistakenly held notion that *Plaut'dietsch* is funny in itself and is therefore incapable of expressing serious thought. Its use here amply disputes such a specious opinion.

solemn pitch, timbre, and loudness of Saxon 'Low' German, an obsolete dialect of the medieval Flemish and Frisian *Mensche* that derives from the Rhenish fan — specifically, the flatlands of the Vistula Delta in Royal Prussia along the North Sea — an obscure discourse lacking standardized rules for grammar. Mind the strain within *dee Enjelsch* to represent the folksy prosody of *dee Plaut'dietsch*.

This note is meant to direct your attention to an esoteric school of thought regarding characters and those figures through which they speak. Certain speakers within this collection thrust contractions toward postulated readers to denote societal dominance, while simultaneously using ligatures to indicate domestic mastery. For example, when the protagonist, who goes by the appellation Roman, says "he'll" rather than "he will," he gives his word, only to impose his will a moment later. Such semantic manipulation indicates nothing less than a masculine imposition upon diction, forcing elision with an adhesive apostrophe. In accordance with that linguistic predilection, I render the title of this exhumed volume as a one-word phrase, "he'll." Furthermore, when Mrs. Dærksen-Dycksche signs her last will and testament, she hyphenates her maiden and married names to assert that she is not chattel. Moreover, by spelling her surname with an "æ," she coaxes out the feminine feature of a ligature, coercing the viscous letters "o" and "e" to coalesce. As a fevered prescriptivist, I typically favour conventional punctuation and spelling rules, yet I try to honour the wishes of a poet in the old, romantic sense of a *Dichter*, by assigning a typographical character to every woman with a speaking role.

I pray this prolegomenon has not brayed for too long. Reading pseudo *Künstlerroman* demands you peer through the sensibilities of its anonymous writer as well as my own, say, environmental sensitivities. While you turn to this portrayal, this prosaic betrayal of the Korneelius "Roman" Dyck fellow, his duplicitous kinsmen, his hypocritical brethren, know the last word is yours.

NATHAN DUECK

Nov. 20, 2006, Rat River, Manitoba

APOSTROPHE

O reader of style; I'll digest typeset,
 'll dine n punct ati n, r pine f r
ink   drop   lets post phe,

O reader of stylo — you'll congest print —
you'll st-r up -ppet-te — -r hung-r for
pin-____ in___pret_tions — __phen —

O reader of stylus: We'll egest script.
We'll urge re·gurg·i·ta·tion; or yearn fr.
pel . . . ver . . . drop . . . : per.

               ,   '   ,
      ,   ,
                                ,

                      —   —
               —
      -              —   —

           .   .
                    .   .

BOOK I

THE HEEL HE HURT WHILE FLEEING HELL WILL HEAL IN TIME

THE ARGUMENT

Roman carried letters for a Mennonite settlement where dust sweeps into the Eastern corner of Manitoba, known as Rat River, a.k.a. *Raut Riefa*. The name of our quiet village (a post office at the R.R. crossing, the windmill silo that was converted into a church, and a convalescent home, all along one paved road) is fictive.

Rumours blew through this dry town after his body was found in a mailbag behind the burned out ruins of the P.O. As the windiest mills tell it, our postal worker was buried under piles of unopened mail. It's said the postman was named Korneelius at birth, but nicknamed Eli as a child. It's also said he couldn't handle correspondence written in the Queen's English. For him, each envelope may as well have read "no man," "nomad," or "nada." [2]

What did villagers on Roman's route think about their "post-*Meista*"? An old widow in "Nostalgia Retirement Villa" (who wishes to stay nameless) said that every day "my poor, poor mailman" found her waiting on lawn furniture beside the latched gate in the fence. "One time, he brought me the mail between his lips. *Oba joh*, his pockmarked cheeks bulged with envelopes, dangling like a cock wattle. What was it he said? 'Fall in'? Hmm . . . 'Pollen.' Was that it? 'Pollution?' I could not make it out."

A retired midwife (who, at five-and-fifty, claims to be too young for retirement; name withheld by request) offered to straighten Roman's foot. This stout lady went on, "It was not quite clubbed, but turned. His Achilles. Atrophied. He leaned on a crutch. A lame man. I had an eye out for Mr. Postman. Repeat his name?" One Christian brother long in the tooth was short with me: "Have I earned anything? No-

---
2. Here, the unknown author suffers from pretensions of writing *en Tunge*, in tongues, or *dee Tunge en Back*, tongue-in-cheek. As a rule, he applies *Enjelsch* to resolve the dialectic of *Plaut'dietsch* and *Hüag'dietsch* ur-texts — just as scholars of old used Latin to synthesize Greek. Absurdly abstruse, abstract usage of *daut Dialetjt* was omitted from these pages. Trans.

thing! No. Thing. At all. *Wada'nusch*. Maybe a Cöoperative coupon or two, mind you." Of course, given how much mail Roman stockpiled, this stubborn, ornery believer wouldn't have known whether anyone was writing. A male orderly at the nursing 'home' winked, "I heard one ol' lady call him 'Roman.' All I know is he stumbled about, mumbling psalms. He was more than a little simple."

The oldest lady in Nostalgia was eager to share the story of how Eli came to take another moniker. As she tells it, he was too young to serve when war broke with "those pinko Mandarins," so he lied on his papers. He left for Korea as the Red River overflowed the Rat in 1950. Shortly after his battalion began manœuvres, Roman was injured by another partisan called *"Scheit — oba, sheete,"* she couldn't say, "starts with 'Sch,' or some such thing. I can never remember the name." The younger lady, once trained in midwifery, said the nickname "SHH" was short for Shepard Harold Hamm. Lo and behold, as Roman marched with his whole outfit to the latrine one morning, SHH busied himself while in line. He bent a Jungle Carbine on his knee to feed a knotted rag on a wire hanger into the bolt tube and through the barrel. After sighting the service rifle named Constance for the newlywed he left, he touched the rusty carpenter's nail hanging on a chain at the nape of his neck. SHH mouthed his creed, "for this one crucified the good Lord," and made a heel turn. He slipped a shell into the casing, with the enemy army engrained in mind, and slid one palm along his muzzle — *K-KRACH*! "Holy Aitch!?!" rang falsetto a stall over. "*Nä.*" Roman was practicing a special number in common time from *das Gesangbuch* [See page 17 for a liturgical dirge with that signature — Trans] when he hurled foodstuffs and his palm sank to his right ankle. He dropped like a dowsing rod. After awakening from a tetanus shot he gawked out the window while seas swelled into quarter sections swaying with prevailing Westerlies.

Who can say why Roman hoarded letters? No one knows for certain. They say this tenderfoot was not man enough to make the rounds. His heel just couldn't hack it.

WHEN THIS PROTAGONIST SAYS "HE'LL" RATHER THAN "HE WILL,"
HE GIVES HIS WORD, ONLY TO IMPOSE HIS WILL A MOMENT LATER

              Enroute to a nursing 'home' for naysayers,
              he'll stagger, gait stutter through gates.

Lurch.
              he will : *hee woat* :: **he'll** : *woat'ee*?

              His steeped dickey, tea-dyed livery, sepia
              buttons tainted by canine urine and fæces.

March.

              He'll overhear rifle fire or falling bomb-
              shells ring tinnitus out of inner earshot.

                                      bellicose mongrel
                                      latrine scavenger
                                      doggerel apologue

              A town crier-cum-letter peddler hums hymns
              of damn lamentation put in layman's terms.

A RAT SWALLOWING ITS TAIL

                    tress limp
           Dyck
                  louse seed
           lies
                  duvet but-
                                een Roos

'You haven't had a night'

                  bosom mat-
           lewd
                  tress mite
           Dick
                  bloat seep
                                bleajcht

                  rouse moth
           Dyke
                  linen mis-
           laid
                  tress lout
                                dee Hütint [3]

---

3. There exists no word in sober-minded *Plaut'dietsch* for 'tattoo.' Unable to render an appropriate term, the unknown author uses *enn'schwiene*, which means 'to dirty,' *hüt*, 'to skin,' and *sindje*, 'to sin,' which should raise the hackles of every native speaker. The portmanteau 'skin-ink' is more agreeable than the cumbersome, verbose neologism 'epidermal pigmentation.' Trans.

Tab   Tab   Tab   Tab   Tab   Tabs set →

   Cellar foams   culvert thaws   ditch
froths   spill
over   Flood of 50
April | May | June

                '. . . 'til you've had a Mennonite.'

                                            Unclr.

   Snake broods
scramble sandbag steppes
Sturm und Drang   Pool elevators
barns   bins brew sloughs

             Salmonellosis: anaerobic bacteria
               from contamination of breeding vermin.
               Isolated in 1877.

Nospacebar

Prediluvianwheyspume
   Straw bale   Rhubarb stalk   Fungal
spray   Blossom spoor   Algal
bloom posy

             Legionella pneumophila: aerosol bacteria
               from contamination of unclean water.
               Isolated in 1976.

Locked SHIFT

    I AM // I CAN // I WILL

PROEM

    He will qwerty homily, you know. Eli will.
                                                                Peck
keys of a manual typewriter
                          over an ad from page
656 of the 1979 *Sears* catalogue. Or a recipe on
page 13 of the *Mennonite Treasury*. Full stop —

Mechanical harmonics scale:
                            Tabs set →
                                       Unclr.
No space bar.
        Locked shift.

[Signed 'Mrs. Dærksen-Dycksche'

version executed FEBRUARY 27/83
STANDARD typeface on REMINGTON]

VODA PREACHES FROM A PULPIT & KORNEELIUS PRAYS FROM A PEW

Dear G-d. Our F-ther in Heaven. Good L-rd. You know. What
am I? A rebel. Yet I swore my life to You. My death, too.

AS PREACHER D— DRONES ABOUT THE SOLDIER IN *LUKAS* VII WHO

You must grow weary hearing petitions from unclean swarms
serving you through what they refuse to do: take up arms,

ASKED CHRIST TO HEAL A SERVANT, HIS THOUGHTS STRAY TO ONE

toss back schnapps, &c. Those olive-branchers turn swords
to ploughshares. My old man, my lay minister, ignores the

CALF WHO CHRISTENED HIMSELF 'ROMAN D' TO FIGHT IN N KOREA

full gospel message. Saving souls. Ours, not Yours, L-rd.
He proclaims the Holy Name, but will not declare pacifism

LONE SON INFANTRY MAN-OF-WAR VS. HIS OLD MAN-OF-THE-CLOTH

the vanity of vanities. Do I speak in vain? Are we Menno-
or Mahatma-nites? Are we men? No! Time to free this will.

GESANGBUCH DER MENNONITEN

148.   Von der Ausbreitung des Evangeliums

Matth. 8, 12. *Aber die Kinder des Reichs werden augestoßen in de äußerste Finsternis hinaus, da wird sein Heulen & Zähneklappen.* [4]

Nach der Weise: Wie soll ich Dich empfangen   Melchior Teschner, 1613.

Key C

```
      G    G    A    B    C     C    E    D    C    C    B    C
  C   D    E    F    F     E/   E    G    G    E    F    D    E

1.Der Du   zum  Heil er   -schienen Der  al  -ler -ärm -sten Welt
  Und von  den  Che -ru   -bi  -nen Zu   Sün -dern dich ge  -sellt;
2.Da -mit  wir  Kin -der  wür -den, Gingst du vom Va  -ter  aus,
  Nahmst auf dich un -sre Bür -den  Und  bau -test uns ein  Haus.

  E   G    C    C    D    G/A   G    C    B    C    A    G    G
  C   B    C    F    D    C     C    C    G    A    F         C

  C/D E    E    D    C    G/A   G    B    C    G    A    A    G    G/F
  G   G    G    G    A    E/F#  E    G    E/F# E    G    F#   D    D

  Den sie  mit  fre -chem Stol -ze  Ver -höhnt für sei -ne  Huld, Als
  Von We  -sten und von   Sü   -den, Von Mor -gen ohne Zahl Sind

  C B C    C    B    E    D/C   B    G    C    D    E/DC B    G
  E D C    E    G    C    D     E    E    A    B    C D  G    B

  E   G    A    G    G/F  E     G    A/B  C    C    B    C
  C   E    F    E    D    C     E    F D  C    D    D    E

  Du  am   dür -ren Hol -ze    Ver -söhn -test ih -re   Schuld!
      K  -KRACH!   Hol-y?    Hell!

  G   C    C    C    G/B  C     C    AG   G    F    G    G
  C   C    F    C    B/G  A     C    F    E    D    G    C
```

                                        Albert Knapp, 1798-1864.
---
4. 'But the children of the kingdom shall be cast out into outer darkness: there shall be weeping and gnashing of teeth' (*Authorized Version*). With this musical annotation malarkey, along with that low-key transposition cacophony on page 19, the unknown author hints that he developed a radio code from *Plaut'dietsch* for Allied Forces in Korea. Intelligence cancelled the project in fear he conversed with Soviets versed in an obtuse dialogue. Trans.

G-d lives. G-d remains alive.
& grammar is dead.

We have killed it.

TRANSPOSITION OF A *HÜAG'DIETSCH* SONG INTO *PLAUT'DIETSCH*,
WARBLED BENEATH HEAVENS PUNCTUATED WITH ASTERISKS, UNDER
THE INFLUENCE OF ANÆSTHETICS PLIED BY A M⋆A⋆S⋆H SAWBONES

Key B
```
         F#    F#    G#    A#    B       B    D#    C#    B     B     A#    B
   B     C#    D#    E     E     B/      B    D#    C#    B     B     A#    D#

0. E34   E7    a7j   Y38o  34    -wdy83h3h    E34   qo    -o34  -q4j  -w53h  23o5
   7he   f9h   e3h   Dy3   -47   -g8   -h3h   A7    W7h   -e34h e8dy  t3    -w3oo5;

1. Eq    -j85  284   I8h   -e34  274   -e3h,  T8htw5 e7   f9j   Fq    -534  q7w,
   Hqyjw5 q7r  e8dy  7h    -w43  G74   -e3h   7he   gq7   -53w5 7hw   38h   Yq7w.

   D#    F#    B     B     C#    F#/G# F#    B     A#    B     G#    F#    F#
   B     A#    B     E     C#    B     B     B     F#    G#    E           B


   B/C#  D#    D#    C#    B     F#/G# F#    A#    B     F#    G#    G#    F#    F#/E
   F#    F#    F#    F#    G#    D#/E  D#    F#    D#/E  D#    F#    E     C#    C#

   E3h   w83   j85   r43   -dy3j W59o-a3      F34   -y9yh5 r74  w38   -h3   Y7œ,  Qow
   F9h   23    -w53h 7he   f9h   W7    -e3h,  F9h   J94   -t3h  9yh3  aqyo  W8he

   B A# B      B     A#    D#    C#/B A#     F#    B     C#    D#/C#B A# F#
   D# C# B     D#    F#    B     C#    D#    D#    G#    A#    B C# F#    A#


   D#    F#    G#    F#    F#/E  D#    F#    G#/A# B     B     A#    B
   B     D#    E     D#    C#    B     D#    E C# B      C#    C#    D#

   E7    qj    e74   -43h  Y9o   -a3   F34   -w9yh-53w5  8y    -43   Wdy7œ!
         Why'd I     nail  my    own   he    -ill?!?

   F#    B     B     B     F#/A# B     B     G#F#  F#    E     F#    F#
   B     B     E     B     A#/F# G#    B     E     D#    C#    F#    B
```

nä

in lieu of flowers, make donations to Mennonite Collegiate Institute.

'The wealth appears to you . . .'
KORNEELIUS "ROMAN" DYCK (b. 17 July 1935) has inherited his reward of heavenly glory. Mr. Dyck, a veteran of the Korean war, had been missing for two years since the transition of the federal postal operator to *Canada Post / Postes Canada* in 1981. He died a union member of good standing in the Post Office Department for the Government of Canada.

To honour his years of loyalty to the Dominion of Canada, a service *in memoriam* will be held on Saturday afternoon at Silo Mennonite Mission, 13 Gutenthal Road. Please remember Mr. Dyck at your family altar as he eats one last meal with his Saviour in heaven.

Village Post Monday, Feb. 28, 1983

LAST POST

TPR. SHEPARD HAROLD HAMM, aged 26, was killed in action on 25th of April 1951 during the Chinese infiltration of Kap'yong Valley. He was buried under the flow of the Pukhan River.

Trooper Hamm was living in Rat River when the war in Korea began. He came to Silo to serve with PPCLI 2nd Battalion. His unit was awarded a distinguished unit citation (US) and a presidential unit citation (Kor). Surviving is his spouse, Constance.

Tangled ĩkxeɓywsvt¢r/ožkxews

   Fatigued recruit
wireless operator smote his
own homemade tattoo
ɖa ʌrɖaʚt wsƧwɖaɵlɵlƟoƧwʚiʜnʈg ʚiʚtws ʚtɖaʚiɵl

Loosen ed car riage

   Shel l shoc ked ob jector
glad rube
brother *Doppelgänger* one bunk over
scoffed off all protocol

                        773 407 734
                        SH HAMM
                        MEN   O/RH/POS
                        CDN FORCES CDN

   Colonel urged on   Shut it
Shitheel brooded
   The rustic sobriquet stuck
Shh . . . for short

                        773 407 734
                        SH HAMM TPR
                        MEN
                        CDN FORCES CDN

   Shh . . . knelt in prayer
triggered regulation rifle no 5
shot himself
can | john | head

— April 1951

To <u>Constance Hamm, Mrs</u>.
    INSERT NAME HERE

We regret to inform you that your husband, <u>Shepard Harold</u>
                                                        INSERT NA-
<u>Hamm, Tpr.</u>, made the ultimate sacrifice for his King and
ME HERE
country. Enclosed are the documents collected among his

personal effects:

22

Say my piece before God and man. Connie
too. I'm a sinner. Sorry. I accept Jesus
Christ as my Lord and Saviour. I want
the blood. I, Shepard Harold Hamm, have
aged to adulthood following the spiritual
guidance of the Silo Mennonite Mission.
May the baptism waters wash my past away.
Please Lord, allow me to hold my peace,
lest I backslide.

        By the time you read my admission it will
be posthumous. So long I have suffered sin-

DIRTIED SEGMENTS
Dirtied segments

MY SCHADENFREUDE
My Roman holiday

  I   Eli   returned
to River of Rat
he Shh . . .
interred in the Pukhan River

ANASTROPHE

   In observance
of circadian rhythms
sun rose with yolk glow
from a candled egg

ENCOMIUM

He will post quires. Testaments or testimonies.

Ice age glaciers carved Pembina Escarpment from prairies to shield, from tree to medicine line.

Lost my place staring at headstone posture of a church minus its steeple. Rows made from felled birchbark with plastic kneelers of summerfallow fertilized by formaldehyde. When Rat River runs off, pews embalm churchgoers in Sunday clothes.

Tangled keystrokes. Loosened carriages. Dirtied segments.

R. Dyck

   [without a return address]

                                        Mrs. Shep
                                         C/O Nos
                                        R.R. 1 St
                                        Rat River
                                        R0A 0T0

EULOGIUM

          P.S. He will punch his negative in woven ribbon
          on black-&-red reversed tape with the typewheel
          weakened 'i' dots & 't' dashes.
                                        What about face
          & what every good boy deserves?
                                        Odes in chords.

          Still, I only comprehend punctuation.
                                        Somewhere
          along the line I lost the plot.
                                        I cannot create
          a tradition.
                      I can only invent a new testament.

ard Harold Hamm
talgia Retirement Villa
n. Main
, MB

APOSTROPHE

Letters are monuments victors inscribe,
grave epitaphs on corpses they inhumed;
Volumes are testaments victims engrave,
scribe epigraphs in your corpus entombed.

```
        re mo            rs

      ph   on          ey

                 t    ic

                    co        d
```

           /ri·mōrs/
-.. .. .. -- .. -. .- - .
                        /fō·nē·
DELTAINDIASIERRASIERRAECHOMIKEINDIANOVEMBERALFATANGOECHO
                               tik/

           /kōd/

                        An æsthetic
  experiment of a lurid phobia based on pathetic
  digressions from lucid philia built in pathology.

ENCODING

The saint in whom G-d takes pleasure is

-.. .. .. -- .. -. .- - .
--. . .-. -- .. -. .- - .
. -..- - . ..-. -- .. -. .- - .

-.. .. .. -- .. -. .- - .
.-. ...- -- .. -. .- - .
-.... --- -. - .. -- .. -. .- - .

.. -. ...- .. ... -. .- ..
--. . .-. -- .. -. .- - .
.... .- .-.. .-.. ... .- ...- .. -. .- - .

.. -. ... . -- .. -. .- - .
-- .. ..-. .... .. -. .- - .
. -.... - . ... -- .. -. .- - .

Götzen-Dämmerung, oder, Wie man mit dem

IN CODEINE

der ideale Kastrat. ° 'ideal eunuch'

DELTAINDIASIERRASIERRAECHOMIKEINDIANOVEMBERALFATANGOECHO
GOLFECHOROMEOMIKEINDIANOVEMBERALFATANGOECHO
ECHOXRAYTANGOECHOROMEOMIKEINDIANOVEMBERALFATANGOECHO

DELTAINDIASIERRASIERRAECHOMIKEINDIANOVEMBERALFATANGOECHO
ROMEOUNIFORMMIKEINDIANOVEMBERALFATANGOECHO
CHARLIEOSCARNOVEMBERTANGOALFAMIKEINDIANOVEMBERALFATANGOECHO

INDIANOVEMBERCHARLIEALFAROMEONOVEMBERALFATANGOECHO
GOLFECHOROMEOMIKEINDIANOVEMBERALFATANGOECHO
HOTELALFALIMALIMAUNIFORMCHARLIEINDIANOVEMBERALFATANGOECHO

INDIANOVEMBERSIERRAECHOMIKEINDIANOVEMBERALFATANGOECHO
MIKEALFACHARLIEHOTELINDIANOVEMBERALFATANGOECHO
ECHOXRAYTANGOECHOROMEOMIKEINDIANOVEMBERALFATANGOECHO

Hammer Philosophizes by Friedrich Nietzsche.

POSY OF ORIENTAL SYMBOLS WHICH RESEMBLES HORIZONTAL APOS-
TROPHES OR POSSIBLY COMMAS COUPLING ON CLEAN WHITE SHEETS

```
der - let - ter - pol - len - pow
let - ter             - pow - der
ter - p                 er - let
pol -                      - ter
len              et - te    pol
pow -         - t      l - len
der - l    r -          - pow
let    er - po          der
ter -                  - let
pol - le              t - ter
len - pow -         ter - pol
pow - der - let - ter - pol - len [5]
```

---

5. Here, the unknown author commits a forgivable solecism, expressing the concept 'poetry' as *derjche dee Bloom räde* rather than *dee Dijcht'konst*. He simply overlooked the ring that distinguishes 'posy' from 'poesy,' like a stigma differentiating pistil from stamen in flowery organs. The *ur*-texts read *dee Breif dee Bloom be'faule*. A literally faithful rendering, 'disseminate germinate exterminate,' forms florid, yet inscrutable, poesy.

TRANSCODING

>   who can bear it. no witness to our footfalls
for we never met. the apnea dawn regiment flushed out a
flood valley winding into seoul. 2nd battalion defended
hill 677 along south flank of a foxhole militia. patter
from a mortar shell churned butterfat and drained blue-
milk flesh. milquetoast. gritteeth file. fall in

>   two cocky cheeks **59 dy33i6 d9di l l l**

rode haemorrhoids raw on benches like pews in messhall.
refused provision to prevent heaving special army meat-
loaf overboard. the torsos of imperialist britons sound
clawhammers around a castiron vessel hull. disseminate.
a slaughterhouse profane. gasps scarce air. coat husked

>   nowhere
now i know. hunkered at the foot of a table. the noise-
less portable typewriter. rationed onionskin. excavated
terracotta outfit. timid. weakkneed row. falling

>   suicide

voided my bowels in gust of swale. a sick mumble heaved
sawteeth over the head of our bunk. germinate. the brim
of buglers pealed calls before morn. talcum moustaches.
pained a pigsticker. grasps bayonet spear. pelt notched

>   why lie
while i cowered in a bunker underfoot. upturned a horde
of commie red chinese. plumbbellied line. a fall

>   **59 d9di6 dy33iw** too cheeky cock . . .

axhead. exterminate. bayonets gouged into sooty legions
dead. husk of shrapnel pounded brigades. fibrous sinew.
a paid for campaigner. clasps tendon scar. hide shucked

THE MENNONITE GAME [6]

'What'd ya say?'

               (*snort*)

'Who're ya callin' names, soldier?'

             'I said, "Shit,"'

'That it?'

          '". . . or get outta the shitter."'

'Ya man enough'

              'Come up here'

'. . . to say that to my face?'

             '. . . & pound nails.'

'I'm not the recruit doin' latrine detail.'

              'I'm shinglin','

'No, ya shootin' yer mouth off'

           '. . . not on shitter duty.'

'. . . because ya won't shoot yer rifle.'

             (*farmer's blow*)

'Hand over the hammer.'

---

6. Anybody with borrowing privileges at a good library could, no doubt, easily trace this drama to its Hellenic sources. Here, the unknown author emulates the contrapuntal tone of commentary within classical Greek tragedy. The 'strophe' occurs when the chorus performs versus opposition. Then, the 'antistrophe' occurs when the opposing chorus returns verses. Trans.

                                                    'Sh —'

'I'm gonna crucify ya like the good Lord.'

                                            '. . . ut it.'

'I'm goin' up there.'

                                            'I said —'

'As they say,'

                                            'Eat shit.'

'. . . "Was mich nicht umbringt,'

                'That which does not kill us . . .'

'macht mich stärker."'

                                    'They also say,'

'We'll see how strong y'are.'

                    '. . . "Arbeit macht frei."'

'Hol — who said that?'

                                    'Martin Luther?'

(chortle)

                                            'Nä.'

'Menno Simons?'

'What do y'know about hallowed Mennos?'

'Raised religious.'

'Y'know it.'

'What's the name & rank on ya?'

'Tags say "R Dyck; Trooper." It's Roman to you.'

'Roman? Tell me how'd ya get such a moniker?'

'How'd "SH Hamm; Trooper" get to Korea?'

'Harold Dyck, my father, served.'

'"Hairy Dick," y'mean?'

'That's why he changed it. To Hamm.'

'"Hairy" Hamm is no better. Hate to say it, SH —'

'It's Hal to you.'

'Any chance ya hail from Rat River.'

'Not far from. Yourself?'

'Barely made it out alive. Hallelujah.'

'Say, what kinda name is "Roman"?'

'It was a different time, back then.'

'A better time. Men were men. Hand over the hammer.'

NOTE TENSIONS BETWEEN LANGUAGES YOU HEAR, READ, AND SPEAK
RE: CITATION

          in other words, liturgy.
                      Allergy,
                      ally

          I am : *etj sie* :: I'm : *sie'tj*?

          Monolog
                  neo
     Monophthong
                  eon
     Monosyllabic
                  one   10
                      A lyrical pastoral by mosquitoes
          etj
                or   riposte arytenoid,
                  -al
                                  register.
          Eent
              ooda   gesture
              Horjche
                      to get the gist

                      speak in jest   20

                      spätj em Spoß
          folk
          lore
                                      Dogma:
                                          I am G-d

                                      Gnostic heresy,
                                      not hearsay
                                      per se.

                          Lowgerman,
                          mothertongue   30

          Only a question
of cadence,
                    intonation,
                         & tempo.

     I can : *etj kaun*

                              round here,
                                   'heal'
                         is pronounced, *heehle*.
               e.g.,
                    'say in a word and   40
                    my servant will be healed.'

                    Evangelium Lukas VII, vii &

9. Da aber Jesus das hörte, verwun-
   er sich über ihn, und wandt
      nd sprach zu dem Volk,
      folgte: Ich sage euch: S
   auben habe ich in Israel nicht
   n.

                              Schwa:
     I identify with neither
     the idealist's idiolect   l i.e.
     nor an idiot's ideology   n e.g. ate

[PHR]   **Aye**
     aye

               Mutta'sproak,
               Voda'launde   50

```
            yule lack
            icon tact
                        aisle faux
            mnemonics   cuss scope
                                    wheel con
                        pneumonics  sin trait

                                    pneumonia
```

I will : *etj woa* :: I'll : *woa'tj*?

                                    signing each letter
                                      'Yours truly,' or
                                        'Sincerely,'
is hard
        lacking verbal moods to connote the tense:
          conditional, indicative, or subjunctive.
A written
                                        system.

                        Witzig, yet without

                        a whit *der Weisheit*

                        Highgerman,
                        fatherland

RE: ITERATION

        Begs the question
of carriage,
                modulation,
                          & signal.

    you can : ***dü kaunst***

transmitting messages
with the salutation
'O' & 'M' for
'old man' or 'old-timer'
                              is hard
lacking a noun case to denote possession:
                              genitive.

                    Apostelgeschichte X,

1.   ein Mann zu Cäs-
area,   Namenn ▮▮▮elius, ein
Haupt   von der Schar, die da heißt
   italische,
    gotselig und gottesfürchtig samt
     ganzen Hause, und gab dem Volk
      Almosen und betete immer zu
Gott.
                   '3. He saw a vision
evidently about the ninth hour of the day an angel of
G-d coming in to him, and saying unto him, Korneelius.'

[PHR]   **Di-**
    dit di-dit

                Tele'graum,
              Brooda'schauft

too incoherent for words.
    Inchoate,
       chaotic

you will : ***dü woascht*** :: **you'll** : ***woascht'ü?***

Dialog
      tow
Diphthong
      wot
Disyllabic

              An idyll libretto   100
dü
   verb   wry post   ,
     -al

Twee

   Vetale

      surely you jest

      sejcha dü Spoß

  tale

     Morsecode,
     brotherhood   110

RESUSCITATION / RE: CESSATION

             Pose a question
of amplitude,
                    undulation,
                            & frequency.

    we will : *wie woa* :: **we'll** : *woa'wie*?

    Trialog
          there
   Triphthong
         ether
Polysyllabic   120

              A bucolic oratorio
  wie
       nas   ripe host   ,
        -al

Dree

       Frodem

                         AGT-PRO

  no word for a call sign.
             Sine wave,
             sinusoidal   130

  i.e.,
     'And a voice spoke to him again the second
time, "What G-d has cleansed you must not call common."
This was done three times.'
                       Apostelgeschichte x, xv
                             & xvii-xxxiii

Petrus sich in sich
merte, was das Gesicht
er gesehen hatte, siehe,
ten die Männer, von ~~Kornel~~i-
~~us~~ gesandt, nach dem Hause Sim
und standen an der Tür;
18. reifen und forschten, ob Simon
dem Zunamen Petrus, allda zur
berge wäre.
19. Indem aber Petrus nachsann ü
das Gesicht, sprach der Geist
Siehe drei Män
20. aber
und zieh mit
nicht; denn ich
21. Da stieg Petrus hinab zu den
die von ~~Kornelius~~ zu ihm
waren, und sprach: Siehe,
den ihr sucht; was ist
arum ihr hier sied?
~~aber sprachen:~~ Roman,
~~ion, a just man, and one~~
~~eth G d, and of good report~~
~~the nation of the Jews, was~~
~~G d by an holy angel to~~
~~into his house, and to~~
~~thee~~.
er sie hinein und be-
sie. Des anderen Tages zog
Petrus aus mit ihnen, und etliche
Brüder von Joppe gingen mit ihm.
24. Und des andern Tages kamen sie
gen Cäsarea ~~Kornel~~elius aber wartete
auf sie, und hatte zusammenerufen
seine Verwandten und Freunde.
25. Und als Petrus hineinkam, ging
ihm ~~Kornel~~elius etgegen, und fiel zu
senen Füßen und betete ihn an.

26. Petrus aber richete ihn auf und
sprach: Stehe auf, ich bin auch ein
Mensch.
27. Und als er sich mit ihm besp-
rochen hatte, ging er hinein und
ihrer viele, die zusamengekommen
ren.
28. Und er sprach zu ihnen: Ihr
est, wie es ein unerlaubtes Ding ist
einem jüdischen Mann, sich zu
Fremdling;
gezeigt, keinen
unrein zu

29. Darum   nicht ge-
weigert zu kom   als ich ward
hergefordert. So frage ich euch nun,
warum ihr mich habt lassen fordern?
30. ~~Kornel~~elius sprach: Ich hab vier
Tage gefastet, bis an diese Stund
und um die neunte Stunde betete ich
in meinen Hause. Und siehe, da stand
ein Mann vor mir in ein hellen Kleid
31. und sprach: ~~Kornel~~elius, dei
Gebet ist erhört, und deiner Almos
ist gedacht worden vor Gott.
32. So sende nun gen Joppe
herrufen einen Simon, mit
men Petrus, welcher ist
in dem Hause des Ger
dem Meer; der wird,
mit dir redden.
33. Da sandte ich vo
dir; und du hast wohl
gekommen bist. Nun sind
gegenwärtig vor Gott,
alles, was dir von Gott
ist.

'"Die Länge trägt die last."'

'Time heals life's tribulations.'

KORNEELIUS DYCK
LIES HERE

A ONE-SIDED CONVERSATION OVER A CROSSED PHONE-LINE, OVER-
HEARD, NOTATED, & RELATED BY AN ANONYMOUS PARTY TO TRANS.

FILE # 770-01-4266
Rat River, MB

'It is a bad word. Not a swear word. But confusing. *B-r-e-i-f-e*. *Dee Enjelsche* spell it that way?'
A.
'How does it give that word — what is it? How did you even make it out.'
A.
'What was your father to make of that letter?'
A.
'You remember *een Maun*. Why would the English *nebbish* who wrote that letter play the fool?'
A.
'You went off to step with your fellow countrymen like lambs to laughter. With *een Sol'dot* side by each.'
A.
'The letter said Trooper Roman Dyck was "dishonourably discharged" because he refused to shoot a rifle.'
A.
'Traitor or prodigal? We learned you —'
A.
'The mouth on you.'
A.
'So you shunned him? You went "on a sabbatical"?'
A.
'What means that? "Quarantined"?'
A.
'Now you say Mennonites cannot be "quiet in the land"?'
A.
'So what if your father served?'

Q.
'He got religion. Then we married. He had the *chutzpah* to enter the ministry and open a mission for veterans.'
Q.
'*Oba joh*, you were my only begotten son —'
Q.
'Doctor said my womb would not survive another Roman birt — *ooda* a Cæsarean. Something about contractions.'
Q.
'He had a son. Out of wedlock. In Mexico. Weaned off a swine.'
Q.
'He was called *Scheit* — *oba, sheete* — starts with "Sch," *ooda* some such thing.'
Q.
'Your half-brother. Rat bastard. Man . . . it. *Oba*.'
Q.
'*Joh*, they fix *dee Vaspa* like slop in this sty.'
Q.
'But you must eat to keep your strength up. You are dead not.'
Q.
'You you are not *een Sol'dot*. *Nä*! You are only a poor, poor mailman. *Dee Breife'droaga*.'
Q.
'That letter said the remainder of Trooper Dyck's record was expunged. You told your father different!'
Q.
'If there is a plague round here you are a carrier. You brought it from Russia with the other vermin.'
Q.
'And you will deliver us from — what did you say? The "Bolsheviks" in Ottawa? How dare you tell me to bite my Mennonite tongue?'

END OF SIDE 1

MY MENNONITE TONGUE (MUCUS, PHLEGM, SPUTUM)

nasal:
    mucus /myü·kəs/
  Marx & Engels /märks ənd eŋ·gəlz/
    nebbish /ne·bish/

                              Menno' drawl
                              pathos

plosive:
    phlegm /py·legəm/
  Gdańsk, Pl /gə·dänsk pō·lənd/
    chutzpah /kůht·spə/

                              twang'*niten*
                              deep *Je'feel*
                              gag reflexicon

fricative:
    sputum /spyü·təm/
  Shit on a Shingle /es·ō·əs/
    yutz /yəts/

                              pathetisch

glottal stop:
      /hō·lē/
      /hel/
      /wīd ī nāl mī ōn hēl/

COUGH UNPLUG SEPTUM (MUM'S ENEMY, OINTMENT)

PARTIAL TRANSCRIPT FROM RECORDING OF A DISCUSSION EAVES-
DROPPED OVER A PARTY LINE, BETWEEN MRS. DŒRKSEN-DYCKSCHE
&

'Stop picking at that, Eli. It'll never —'
Q.
'Fine. Roman. *Yutz*. Do not look stiff at me.'
Q.
'Watch the words you use. Swears. God above hears you call a ploughshare "evil" *ooda* a sword "dæmonic".'
Q.
'The silo for missiles now stores the grain!'
Q.
'*Joh,* Jesus Christ, lily of the valley, rose of Sharon fair cursed a fig tree.'
Q.
'The tree was *onn'rein* ['unclean' — Trans].'
Q.
'The question is why you would say "proletariat," once yet.'
Q.
'*Dee Mennoniet* have nothing in common with Commies!'
Q.
'*Raut Riefa* is a commune not. We are not Hutterites.'
Q.
'We have nothing in common with that inbred cult.'
Q.
'How dare you say c.o. are the first letters of Communism. What about *dee Forestei*? Or Soviet pogroms!'
Q.
'*Oba joh*, we are Protestants. Not "Comrades." *Düsent!*'
Q.
'Some of us are formed in God's image —'
Q.
'Others are made from scratch.'

A.
'You will say nothing about *een kratjcht Breife*. [7] Who would listen, anyways?'

END OF SIDE 2

---
7. Uncertain translation. The words in italics here are roughly equivalent to the English idiom 'by' or 'to the letter,' indicating the unknown author prides himself on being a 'man of letters.' The next page records several italicized terms in order to please polyglot wigs and pleonast wags alike. Trans.

GLOSSARY

aundra, 'other'   86.
dee Brooda'schauft, 'brotherhood'   38.
Daunz, 'to dance'   86.
dee Dietsch, 'German'   4, 5, 10n, 13n, 17n, 19, 52.
düsent! 'thousand!' an expression of disbelief   46.
dee Enjelsch, 'English'   4, 5, 10n, 43.
fleesch'foawijch, 'flesh / meat-paint'   89.
dee Forestei, 'forestry labour' by conscientious objectors in Russia   46.
Frodem, 'to breathe'   40.
een Gnurpel, 'gristle'   87.
Horjche, 'to hear'   35.
hüag, 'high'   4, 10n, 19.
deep Je'feel, 'feeling'   45.
Joh, 'yes'   10, 44, 46, 84, 88.
dee Launde, 'land'   36, 86.
dee Mennoniet, 'Mennonite'   4, 46, 83.
dee Mensch, 'human beings'   5, 41.
dee Mutta, 'matriarch'   4n, 36, 52, 67.
Nä, 'no,' the term functions as a shibboleth   10, 11, 19, 33, 44, 57-59.
dee Oarm, 'arm'   83.
dee Oasch'loch, 'corn-hole'   86.
oba, 'although!' an intensifying expression   10, 11, 44, 46, 88.
Ope'mül, 'mouth agape' /
  E.g., a motto: *Best du opp'em mul jefolle?*,
  'Did you fall on your mouth?'   86.
plaut, 'low'   4, 5, 10n, 13n, 17n, 19, 52.
een Prädja, 'preacher'   92.
een Roos bleajcht, 'bloody rose'   13.
Sheete, 'shoot'   11, 44.
een Scheit, 'shit'   11, 44.
woo schient'et? 'how shines it?'   83.
dee Schwiene, 'pig'   13n, 86.
Sindje, 'to sin'   13n, 86.
Sinje, 'to sing'   86.
dee Sol'dot, 'soldier'   43, 44.
spott, 'to parody,' an affirmative sense of jest, or a pejorative sense
  of ridicule   87.
dee Sproak, 'language' & / or 'speak'   4n, 36, 52, 86.
dee Täa, 'tar'   86.
dee Tele'graum, 'telegram'   38.
Tjitje, 'to look'   83.
Vaspa, a light meal in the late afternoon   44, 83, 86.
Ve'füle, 'to rot'   86.
Vetale, 'speak'   39.
dee Voda, 'patriarch'   16, 36.
dee Worscht, 'sausage'   86, 88, 91 /
  E.g., a benediction: *Aules haft en Enj; Bloß de Worscht haft twee Enja*,
  'Everything has an end; except sausage — it has two ends.'

CÆSURA

,

BOOK II

ENGLISH ONCE SPELLED HEEL *HÆLA*, HELL *HÆLLE*, & HEAL *HÆLAN*,
LINKING 'A' & 'E' LIKE MEAT CURED AT A MENNONITE FARM.
AT THAT TIME, LOW GERMANS PRONOUNCED THE WORDS
HEEHLE, *DEE HALL*, & *DEE HACK AUM FOOT*,
LINGERING ON EACH 'A' & 'E.'
& WE STILL DO.

ANOTHER NOTE ON THE TEXT

I DEPARTED MY CHILDHOOD HOME AT AN INCIPIENT AGE TO ATTEND normal school in the city of Winnipeg. Upon graduating with a general certificate of education, after studying between rows of codices in a library with more depth than ancient Lake Agassiz, I taught school in Rat River. I took it upon my stooped shoulders to educate the first generation of Mennonites reared without *onsa Mutta'sproak*. Despite the conservative opinions held by their predecessors, none of *dee Wunda'tjinja* on the roll in my "Scriptural Philology" classes feel convicted about *Plaut'dietsch*. The parochial acoustics of our baroque Protestant 'brogue' sound foreign to their tin eardrums. To a scholar responsible for mental inculturation, like the farmer accountable for agricultural cultivation, the question is whether this moribund *Weltschmerz* yields anything honestly ethical, not ethnically false. Some harrow the ground; others furrow their low brows.

The fall of *Plaut'dietsch* wore on me while I translated the second part of "he'll." Although the following pages were not stapled to the canon, a "magnum opus," if you will, I found them in the manila envelope mentioned earlier — riddled with a-forementioned rat 'scat.' Presumably, these loose leaves — *dee Bläda von Grauss* — were composed post-Roman, yet they contain his idiosyncratic nomenclature. The late Shepard Harold Hamm, previously a character without lines, will not appear in Book II. Pages 56-59 explain his absence in part. Notice how the unknown author reinterprets the trope of 'pollen' from Book I. Certain other speakers place unction upon readers to keep English 'pollution' from their mailboxes stacked like beehives marking town limits. For example, when the antagonist Nada says *dee Hall*, rather than Hell, he yearns to preserve the sacred colony, and its communal fellowship, from all profane colonization by the Dominion of Canada. Before you continue deciphering or, better, digesting, keep your pointer finger in place at the second passage entitled 'The Argument,' an homage to the rhetorical or tonal tics of the first. Additional pages of the *ur*-texts are faithfully reproduced, without critical pruning or fertile commentary.

INSTANT 'TRANS-E-LATER!'

Interprets words and phrases from one language to another in the Roman alphabet at the touch of a few buttons . . . and it is a calculator and metric definer, too.

PRESS [PHR] TWICE PLUS LETTER

- A Do you speak
- B How do you say
- C Take me to
- D I am looking for
- E Where is
- F I would like
- G How much
- H Is there
- I What is
- J Is this
- K Will he

50 common phrases programmed into 1 unit. Its 16-figure display scrolls for lengthy passages and comes in 4 colours.

IT'S A GREAT LANGUAGE TEACHER

This ductile computer flashes words in its memory by category (such as houseware or hardware, &c.) and by their frequency of use; it even helps correct spelling, and can clear-up double meanings!

Plastic case: 6 3/4" x 3 1/2" x 1 1/2." Vinyl carrying case includes adapter for use with 110-120v. 60-Hz AC.

ORD.INFO: Order 4AA batteries below.
3 C 1842C — Shp. wt. 2lbs . . . $198.95

THE ARGUMENT

Some suit came to this town about the time Roman turned up dead. He asked around about the mail (was it delivered in a timely fashion, or at all?) but he affected the refined accent of an Englishman, so nobody would talk to him. Local old-timers pretended they couldn't hear his dressed-up lingo and resident youngsters made as though they shouldn't speak it. Without anyone left to bother, this shyster hid out in the rat trap of a post office near where the grid road starts. That was before it burned up, of course. False front and all. He was soon thrown out on his ear. It goes without saying that no one's heard from him since. The well-heeled outsider spouted nothing but genteel twaddle with the royal we.

A phone call to the Postmaster General was no help at all. A lady on the other end, whose voice yodeled over the receiver, said the investigation into our letter carrier's "malfeasance" ended when their officer finally upped and disappeared. As Canada Post tells it, a man who took the alias "Nada" sent only a part of his report to Ottawa. That said, the whining lady told us there was a good reason to believe a government fella sent the file 'in question.'

Later on, a letter showed up at the Rat River P.O. It was sent without a return address, just like the one that lady spoke of. But, in what must've been someone's idea of a joke, it looked to be mailed by "R. Dyck" to "Mrs. Shepard Harold Hamm." Let me tell you, nobody at Roman's memorial service laughed when we opened the envelope only to find paper clippings inside. Some slips were snipped from books by Edgar Allan Poe, Herman Melville, and Nathaniel Hawthorne. A few strips were torn from the "Canada Post Corporation Act" with a handwritten line: NOTHING HAPPENED. I'll say. Then again, according to the powers-that-be, nothing happened that is not there. May as well have said "nix," "naught," and "null." Let the government lady list that in her 'errata.'

CONSOLIDATION

Canada Post Corporation Act

[NOTHING HAPPENED]

INCOMPLETE NOTATION OF FIRST DICTAPHONE TAPE ADDRESSED TO

time will tell whether i finally got hold of myself by ta
of poison and swallowed hard to end it once and for all i
sion of suicide with a tone of voice instead of writing a
sion by some trooper named hal or shh for short before he
in his muzzle to meet his maker i met him one day earlier
ugh see he made his move on me after he found out we both
that cocky sodomite twisted my arm back and then got hold
could not bring myself to march with allied forces in kap
now i get what was going through his mind who wants to gi
with himself after he comes up empty handed i have to say
ll away from that putsch no man could stand such ill will
to go the way he went i must go into the grave hole i dug

REMEDIED GRAMMATICAL ERRORS BY THE SPEAKER OF COARSE ENGL

           coARse

          vulgAR

           jARgon

           ARgot

nä nä nä nä nä nä nä nä nä nä nä nä nä nä nä nä nä

THE POSTMASTER GENERAL WITH REGARD TO THE DEATH OF R DYCK

king my life with these hands if i lifted this coffee mug
get you never heard of me so i am recording a short admis
note once when i was a soldier in korea i took the confes
hooked his big toe around a trigger and tucked the nuzzle
shingling the roof on a shitter shh was asking for it tho
came from rat river which is no place for a shitheel like
of my cheek when i handed over my hammer afterward i just
yong with thoughts fixated on shh shot through the helmet
ve his life when he can take it what kind of man can live
i have no regrets about nailing my own heel to get the he
from his brethren you know why i just cannot bring myself
i honestly believe a lie does in while the truth will out

ISH LANGUAGE TO AVOID OFFENDING THE DISCRIMINATING READER

    lANguage

      slANg

  harANgue

From Songs of No Man

THE TEETOTALER'S RHAPSODY, OR: A RECHABITE TROUBADOUR

While *be'drintjeke* ° scolds, 'la-di-dah,'   the drunk
as though he swears an oath to quit,
he tips back one last hurrah.

***na*-dah *na*-dah *na*-dah *na*-dah *na*-dah *na*-dah *na*-dah *na*-**

His bride curses the habit,
while a band plays, 'oompah-pah,'
as though she stubs her toe — 'dammit.'

dah na-*dah* na-*dah* na-*dah*

                        The
nag pulls on his reins to spit,
while a horse neighs, 'brou-ha-hah.'

na-dah *na*-dah *na*-dah *na*-dah
na-dah *na*-dah *na*-dah *na*-dah

As though he tip-toes home to ma,

na-dah *na*-dah *na*-dah *na*-
dah na-*dah* na-*dah* na-*dah*

                       the
bridle reigns without a bit,
while her gelding temperates. °   *dee von stoatjet*
                                        Je'drintj wajch blift

dah-dah-dah-dah dah-dah-dah-dah-dah dah-dah-dah-dah-

SECOND DICTAPHONE TAPE STARTS AT SOUND OF THROAT CLEARING

take matters into my own hands for good now i had a drink
or two of courage which is just as well because i hear te
ll my halitosis is poisonous not that you could ever know
with my microphone and your speaker between us like a sch
ism or however you say the word from sunday school catech
ism to describe the separation of mennos from one another
my old man my lay minister taught me the truth first hand
time has come to meet my maker all the letters for mother
s day are too heavy to lift i just cannot bring myself to
handle them i will light piles of unopened mail like kind
ling to burn the office please announce my funeral on the
radio as though nothing happened it is all in the telling

THE STACCATO ACCENT CAN BE MISTAKEN FOR ALLERGIC REACTION

Postmaster General Joseph Julien Jean-Pierre Côté assigned a representative from the 'dead letter' office, pseudonymed Nada, to notate the content of a lot along the 49th parallel. Frankly, the assignment became a crying shame, for Nada submitted a report rife with errors. A hearing into his incompetency was halted by the Progressive Conservative Government in 1984. Not one complaint about missing mail was ever filed: either no one offered any grievance, or it never found its way to the Ombudsman's desk. Pursuing the internal code of conduct, the Crown Corporation recommends that another investigation proceed posthaste.

Tpr. Roman Dyck was prevented from bearing the Union Jack into what is now Kap'yong, on the Southern rim of Korea, because his right heel was injured while awaiting deployment with PPCLI (CFB Silo). Tpr. Dyck was dishonourably discharged for refusal to deploy his firearm. The Royal Canadian Artillery dismissed their most errant soldier without decoration. Upon returning to the centre of the province of Manitoba, in the Canadian core, the errand boy hired on as a lowly postal worker at Rat River.

nada Post Corp   ber 16, 1981

andonment of   49. Every per   offence who
ail   unlawfully and   andons, misdi-
                      rects, obstructs,   or detain
                      progress of any mail   mail con

[NADA P. 61]

   Pariah dog gnawed gangrenous rot from abdomen of the deceased. Arms pinioned back. Loins turned. Pigeon-toed. Bled-out tattoo of a rat swallowing its tail (?), on right ankle. A pocket diary; 'SHH' ██████████████.

Just after dark one gusty evening in the autumn of 19—

In reference to Shepard Harold Hamm

Dear Preacher D—,

    I presume that I am not a fool, but then I am a reader of E. A. Poe, which I take to be only one remove from a fool. True, since I have taken residence in a retirement-villa, I may devote myself to many mental discussions of fictional affairs which I neglected after my conversion at an early age; I mean by those words my youthful marriage to a rude man who now peacefully rests in the underwater morgue with other infantrymen fallen in Korea. I look upon my wedding at the age three-and-thirty, after completion of catechism, confession of faith, and my baptism, as something of an unfortunate occurrence. I write to ask permission to admit a best acquaintance or bosom accomplice into my matrimonial bed, the bed abandoned by Shepard Harold Hamm, a trooper who is pacified, presumed quelled, in action. Once he knew the way, but he could not find the way back.

    Good heavens! It is odd how I, a mere widow, am made to live after the fashion of a spinster or sister rather than helpmeet. Simple and odd. It is beyond comprehension how I thus live alone amid absolutely myriad 'oddities.' The fact is, my proposal is very odd indeed, and I have no doubt that we can manage it sufficiently well ourselves; I want to engage with an affair, an affair so simple and without fault or blame, with this one simpleton who delivers my letters. And what, after all, is the matter on hand? Why, I will tell you in these few words in good conscience; but, before I begin, allow me to caution you. This is an affair demanding greatest secrecy, for others should accuse me of forfeiting my salvation, if they knew my designs.

    It grieves me, as a member of your Silo Mennonite Mission, to purge my conscience regarding your teaching widows to suffer unto death in wont of a husband. D—, you who dare all things, are too fond of the cant of indoctrination. Only submission turns oppression to repression? Hogwash! Why did you decide upon putting the lie to your ministry?

I have reason to suspect you have purloined the rhetorical dogma of brother Menno Simons; this is beyond all doubt. Verily, verily, you have forgotten the profound importance of your pulpit. I have heard accounts from deacons that you play the transistor radio, possibly a hand crank, tuned to A.M. 1250, and not only for funeral announcements of the morn. I also hear your other habits are no less profane. What comes next, jocular dancing? Jocund drinking? Fecund wenches? The red light filament of the *Co-op* sign at the gasoline station next door shines on every crepuscular nook of the premises in which it is impossible to discern any meaning at all. Your railing will bring every hardscrabble Mennonite to heel.

   I have an odd notion the messenger, though a lame man, is head over heels. He searched for me everywhere. We will be affectionately struck [*sic!* — Perhaps a circumlocution for 'stricken' or the F-word?] through the entire building, room by room; devoting the nights of a whole week to each. But, in order to proceed without the fear of God, you must bless this affair beyond question.

   Given my druthers, if you do not intervene, I may be moved to make the naysayer of Rat River privy to your secrets. I may become cross. A most senior woman of the rest home, abbreviated 'Œ,' revealed to me the aggressive sacrilege of your transgressions. In light of our faith, your flock would surely mumble after learning you fumbled about the Great War as a soldier who sullied the name 'Hairy Dick.' That was before I called you father-in-law.

   Please know Shepard Harold Hamm cleft our linens without whispering one word of susurration, only whimpering through the shroud as he left. He did me an evil turn, about which I now grumble. It is repugnant sophistry right out of Poe.

   Only Mennonites can be men. I feel this within; everyone is guilty of a *non distributio medii* in thence inferring not all Mennonites are men. Be a man, not a castrate, fool; consecrate my union.

[Signed 'Mrs. Constance Hamm']

WHERE POE WOULD PLACE CONTRACTIONS WERE HE WRITING TODAY:

[PASSAGES UNDERLINED IN "THE PURLOINED LETTER." 1845.]

           "Ha! ha! ha!   ho! ho! ho!
                  "oh, Dupin, you will be the death of me

You will now understand   the
purloined letter
          — in other words

                             You will remember,
            the Prefect laughed
                                  this mystery

        in his possession, he will
                          commit himself
                  His downfall   will not

TRY TO HONOUR THE WISHES OF A POET BY ASSIGNING A TYPO-
GRAPHICAL CHARACTER TO EVERY WOMAN WITH A SPEAKING ROLE

        Inside a decrepit cenotaph to this country's
        birth, an elderly lady aching with nostalgia
        will approach her letter carrier rendezvous.

Crouch.
        she will : *see woat* :: she'll : *woat'ee*?

        She'll encroach on furniture with the emblem
        Œ crocheted in upholstery by mildewy spores,
        her psoriatic girth pouring into nude nylon.

                              bawl incredulous
                              spleen caterwaul
                              glandular curdle

        She'll position her sit upon within varicose
        hosiery of vile mothball odour from a thrift
        store outsiders mock 'Menno Clothes Closet.'

        woe to you man-at-arms
        of lachrymose mien who
        wears bilious demeanor

                      amen

Œ

    Her maidenname
etched in brass
listed on a directory over
looking the convalescent home

> *Fire Regulations Require This Door*
> *Be Kept Closed for Your Protection*

    Sloughing war a stag Harold
Hamm changed
name to the misnomer
Dü etj | Due wick | Dew ick

    Charged *Mädchen*
Ethel take his surname Dyck
  She obeyed that will
  Rues the morn

signing letters Dœrksen Dycksche
Ethel yoked
yet she ribbed
Hal was less than kosher

    Ethel eye
sores satchels of morose
letters until the prodigal darkens
her door peephole

PAEAN

Alterations & amendments made to the statement must cast doubt upon this will.
Who puts faith in each little serif from the electric stencil to liberate her? Will moveable type exonerate?

I, Ethel Doerksen-Dyck, possessor of one sound mind, one resonant memory, must be held solely responsible for my only begotten son's rattle.

Tapping fingers remind me of an English paean:

"To the old rugged cross I will ever be true"

I, a word I now see turn in on itself, myself, if I live within a moment reminiscence touches today, the present relinquishes yesterday.
If, a word I now see turn away from itself, I live for no one, if no one resembles none, if Roman is a semblance of nonce, we are ensemble anon. . . .
I am bound to spell it out. By my oath.

"It's shame and reproach gladly bear / Then"

I helped my son defect. 'Mutta,' he said, 'he- al me.' A plea of defection. 'It is time, no?'

"He'll call me some day to my home far away"

Path is a path is a
path is a path.

Loneliness extreme.

EPODE

The funereal rites for all deceased Mennonites decree that the body of an excommunicated soul be disposed of without ritual ceremony in back forty outside whitewashed fences of a cemetery beside our Mission.

A memorial for my only begotten son was attended by none. No one helped me to inter a charred carcass face down & head West in the oozy field for soldiers who return taxidermied.

Nobody let me save face. Save for Roman.

Prima facie, the cadaver, some John Doe who died from pathogenic bacteria in the water shed of a floodplain, looked like the spitting image, nay, a graven image of Korneelius Dyck.

I cannot go on without coming clean. I claimed the debased trunk from its rest, dressed it in a defiled postal uniform, & set it aflame with in a deserted post office. Because the remains were desecrated by such an immolation, our so-called elder prayed for every sinful infidel & preached on idolatrous ways.

Nowadays, Eli has made his name. His coinage, codename, or coda.

I long for a nomad son to serve me while I lie prone in Nostalgia.

O can Nada stand on guard?

TELEPHONE 728-6378
AREA CODE 204

RURAL ROUTE 1
STN. MAIN

NOSTALGIA RETIREMENT VILLA
RAT RIVER, MANITOBA
R0A 0T0

THE RETIREMENT-VILLA.
INTRODUCTORY TO *DEE HALL*.

It is worth remarking that — though disinclined to detail the eventualities that landed me for a season in hell, this broken 'home,' or *dee Heim*, my pious compatriots term *dee Hall* — a tendency toward awkward auto-biographical self-flagellation has twice possessed me while addressing the public. The first time was thirty-one or two years ago, when I favoured a piteous audience — inexcusably, and for no earthly reason, regaling attitudinal young and attentive elderly alike — with anecdotes regarding a life that led me from the icy din of the community of Tyndall over yonder to the halcyon quietude of this retirement-villa, here. Now — due in part to a general degradation of civilization writ large, I assume, I was unable to reach out to more than a rare listener — I again grasp the public's collars, and exhale a vague rant to grip my fellow residents of Dutch extraction, let us not say 'patients' or 'pilgrims,' in this facility. As they tend to trill in coarsest English, I dwell *een Darp*, meaning in a 'village.' They also say *villa*, meaning 'lowborn,' or *prost*, 'common,' possibly downright 'crass.' Say what thou shalt, 'Nostalgia's' library's shelves of hardbound American literary classics would likely overwhelm the stock of any lesser 'shtetl.' I am well on my way to the peasant's education in this, my ramshackle one-room school-house. With my introductory remarks I pursue the infamous lead of *The Scarlet Letter*. That novel was published the very year that my puritanical forebears arrived on American shores. The truth seems to be that, after Hawthorne absorbed his nineteenth-century society, he addressed, not the many readers who toss aside their Yankee hanky romances, or those who lack the temerity to take those weighty titles from the shelves, but few of us migrants who comprehend his adulterous characters.

Indeed, previous wordsmiths have aspired to far greater eloquence than this rheumatoid agonist or arthritic rhetor, and so they entertained their audiences with such depths of convention as could fittingly be shewn; as though the printed word, once loosed at large, would complete an aura of holiness by bringing thine scribe into communication with those mendicant infantrymen swinging death's scythe. Those with more cosmopolitan tastes wilt yearn to hear sighs of great masters in the pages of this composition.

   The Christliest words in red are the frozen and benumbed utterances of the resurrected Lord rendered in His Holy Word forever! This auto-biographer means to stand in some discernable relation with her foremost audience, the risen saviour, to seek pardon for all the routine sins and other sundry carnalities that risk exposing a soul like virgin topsoil to alkali of forgetfulness at the conclusion of this rude bawdy's [*sic* — This malapropism or malodious wordplay is not in keeping with the bland expository tone of Hamm's tome. Quite possibly crude 'brutality' or brusque 'cruelty'?] macabre putrefaction.

   The present epistle lends itself to each of us as the scintillating intercourse of Christ with whom I entered into crimsoned correspondence. Thou shalt endeavour to tell the curious memories of old-folk dying out like umlauts in this spurious of a separatist burg. At the very least we do not live in a secular sect like those Catholics. Caution to the holier-than-thou reader that this pigment does not imprint his thumbs, unless he longs for a smudged inheritance all his own. Prithee, friend, leave me alone with thy patience.

[Circa MCMLXX]

HAWTHORNE WOULD PLACE CONTRACTIONS HERE WERE HE WRITING:

[PASSAGES UNDERLINED IN *THE SCARLET LETTER*. 1850.]

                  thou shalt never know!

      Thou wilt not reveal his name?

thou wilt

        yonder man."

                         thou shalt tease me as thou wilt

                    cried Hester,
                      "Let God punish! Thou shalt

                    leave it all behind

                            thou wilt see her

        But thou wilt love her dearly

                    and thou shalt sit upon his

knee
        Thou wilt love him — wilt thou not?"

                "Thou thyself wilt

see thy father?   thou shalt know

            now thou wilt?

BREATH HELD
EAR STOPPED

From *Martyrs' Mirror* or *The Bloody Theatre*,

compiled by Thieleman Jansz van Braght, one unsigned, untitled Dutch poem found in that martyrology of defenceless Protestants from *Anno Domini* unto the Year of our Lord, 1660

(Anabaptists John Foxe excised from *Book of Martyrs*)

       ends with a line of Latin quotation

Justus ex fide vivit
                     Just will live by faith

The line

       Till my trophies at last I lay down

from a musical television program *Hymn Sing*

composed by George Bennard, 'The Old Rugged Cross' was sung by a CBC choir on Feb. 27th *Post Meridiem* that Lord's Day of Rest, 1983

(never mind all of the show's Producers are heathen)

I refuse to recite these lines &
I refrain from listening to them
while I whistle past a graveyard

                              Ear stopped
                              Breath held

C/O

Her nomdeplume
addressed the steer
lover who gave their vows
less than short shrift

In care of a conscientious
objector turned postal worker
Shirking condolences
elegy | eulogy | obituary

There is a fine of $5 to $500
for the unlawful removal
of this label.
Trystero (TM)

Nursing *hausfrau*
mourns with rue
yet feels useful as
teats on a barren hog

Busies herself tearing bedsheets
into flag semaphore
until the last scion calls
on her

Constance ear
bashes a tombstone chiseled
SHH epitaph for her headboard
until shadows bow

TRY TO HONOUR THE WISHES OF A POET BY ASSIGNING A TYPO-
GRAPHICAL CHARACTER TO EVERY WOMAN WITH A SPEAKING ROLE

>
> Sulking within a crêpe veil, a stout lady
> will lurk under dander-embroidered doily.

Shroud.
> **she can : *see kaun***
>
> She'll slur rehearsed memos of morose air
> or unrequited missives memorized by rote.
>
>
> phlegmatic
> flesh balm
>   melancholy
>   rash salve
>
>
> After letches, wretches, or leery voyeurs
> chide about the cubic zirconia jewelry on
> her eczematic ring finger, she'll linger.
>
>   florid verb & / or
>   choleric predicate
>
>   a Menno oblate
> omen

Nostalgia Retirement Villa
R.R. 1 Stn. Main
Rat River, MB
R0A 0T0

September 17, 1972

Postmaster General Joseph Julien Jean-Pierre Côté
Whither Canada?

Dear Sir:

I have noticed that a pigeon is seldom caught unawares. By nature, that ubiquitous genus, *Columbidae*, has brought ordinary men into contact with what would seem diabolical 'coo'-ing and odious, shall we say, stool, about which I have no space to waste. I long to speak of a postman, a mere messenger pigeon, under your employ. I have grown familiar with the murmuration of pigeons after years of verdant leisure, and could relate divers tales of these dove-cousins, were I so moved, at which aged men would grin spittle and take delight in spite of their toothless gums. But I waive that grim satisfaction to address one pigeon's death, an end as strange as any I e'er saw or heard of. While of other fowl, a magpie or what have you, I might shrive about continual agitation or nearly complete apathy, of this nuisance especially I strive to describe nothing of that sort. A pigeon of such arcane caricature was struck dead by one of your mailmen fleeing duty, and furthermore its fetid carcass smote the dandruff from a gentlewoman who fled said postman. She was the first of those two birds brought down by one stone.

Ere holding forth on the enigmatic incident as it unfolded before astonished orbs, I must elaborate upon your wrong-doing, your wrong-headed postman, your egregiously wrong-footed postal clerk, and my hand-wringing.

The accosted crone, who cannot conceive how closely she mirrors the famous actress Ethel Merman for she abhors that indulgent vanity of picture shows, corresponded daily with her descendants about her profound advice for a long life. Hence, though she belongs to an advanced age which is proverbially lax and listless, even to the point of lethargy, she waits on the daily rounds of your postman in her recalcitrant ignorance. For a woman of her Mennonite lineage, with its attendant social morals and cultural mores, doing nothing often leads her to feel almost wholly useless, or even less useful than that. The rude business was done to my neighbour lady by a pigeon while she pursued your postman. The curmudgeonly victim, a personage little given to any poetic grousing, failed to restrain herself from pronouncing a solitary cuss word. She did not speak vaingloriously, but to simply comment, plainly, 'I would prefer not t—,' as she was stricken full on the jowls by an ill-tempered winged rat. That was an insouciant turn of phrase, I attest, that she loved to repeat, for the surfeit of it perfectly suited the cowardly indignation of her Anabaptist convictions regarding feckless, fist-clenched pacifism. But what of the impotent war they wage against armed aggression?

   Well after the period at which this pithy tale begins, the old woman implored that I, her tattler, foul [*sic* — Conceivably 'fondle' as in 'maul'? Or, feasibly, 'molest'?] these pages to craft a letter of mewling complaint in my pidgin English on her behalf. The beguiled hag, who was almost laid waste in her caducity, beseeched me to beg remuneration for she can no longer cluck along with her plucked cursive quill.

   I am, etcetera.

MELVILLE WOULD PLACE THESE CONTRACTIONS INTO HIS WRITING:

[PASSAGES UNDERLINED IN "BARTLEBY, THE SCHRIVENER." 1853.]

                              in his passivity
                                              he will

                  fall
                       and then
he will be rudely treated,

                       "You *will* not?"
                       "I *prefer* not."

                       he will
                       "Bartleby!"

              he will not budge.

                     budge?   he will *not* be a
                     vagrant

                              Since he will not quit
                   me,   I will change

```
        Société canadienne          tes — 16 October 1981

    struction of    53. Every per    ommits an offence who
    cords           knowingly secret  stroys, mutilates,
                    obliterates, defac erases or changes
                    any record or ac     transaction
                    pertaining to           Corpo-
                    ration, or ref        or deliver
                    such record o              au-
                    thorized off
                    demand.
```

[NADA P. 79-80]

Recorded for posterity.

1. Motel Gideon's Bible. Dog-eared pages. Inscription within front cover. Partly legible longhand:

    SOS   I made water
  on tiled cavities   ulcerated wallpaper
  mirrored cataracts
    Radio silence   patois

    Notion wearied
  seamstress mistress poked her
  own homespun tattoo
  a rose of sharon fair

Remainder of frontispiece, torch in an urn, shorn to Roman numerals of ages yore ~~for rereading. High/Low German, for postal mortem~~.

●. ~~"Instant 'Trans E Later!'"~~

APOSTROPHE

No one need worry about a chilly
supper with the *Tupperware* family
of plastic sepulchers for leftovers
or burped microwavable cadavers.

O, she said, what on earth, laborious
Mennonites have gone the way of bourgeois
collector spoons in a silverware drawer;
scattered . . .

. . . at random among the public.
What kind of man cracks a tin of SPAM
luncheon meat without first turning the key?

```
                D                  C ILL
           I                          MIL
       L  IC     LC           L    V
          D MIC      V  L  C D V


               ID                L    I
   M    I      V                            I
   C LL C            I       ILV        D
      C     D


                  D M  M           LIC
          I D    M  C  C       I       M
   L  C      M      I        I       I
```

                                              ARTICLE OF FAITH

The

is   determiner that refers to a person who is distinct.
   A

      is less definite,
                        but it remains   article of faith.
                                       An

                                is least definitive,
but it remains articulate about
                                       ism.
                                   a
                                    the

                /rek·tō/   /hēl/   /fütstül/   /pid·jən/   /fō/

/vər·sō/   /pid·jən/   /hōlē/   /hel/   /hir·ō/

He

is a pronoun   used to represent a male or any person.
          That

              is more relative,

                          but   remains pronounced.
                              It

                              is the most objective,

but remains a

                    cement.
                pro
                  noun

          Pronouncement:

                        Compose the figure of speech
used to represent an action,
                            happening,
                                  or state of being
mentioned earlier in the discourse.

                              Find the way to say a
proverb.

PROVERB

CATASTROPHE: AD DRESS

SCENE 1. The Retirement-Villa, comfortably and tastefully rococo, is divided into sections, or homesteads, each square in shape, housing a number of residents between its stuccoed walls and below its asphalt roof. The following episode occurs inside a wood-paneled cafeteria between homesteads. Two elderly ladies sit at a round Arborite table at their assigned seats in front of the serving buffet that extends from a stack of trays to an urn serving cold coffee (dee kolt Koffe) *in ceramic mugs. The dining area contains bookshelves with assorted hardbound American literary classics and various porcelain tchotchkes. The plastic-wrapped chesterfield beneath a framed print constitutes a waiting area, stage left. At stage right, a door leads out.*

The oldest lady in the rest home, who goes by 'Œ,' crosses her ankles and straightens the lace of her hem. A younger lady, 'C/O,' removes a pocket diary from her pleated slacks and makes a note.

Œ. Eat *Vaspa* before the rats get to it, youngster.

A male orderly enters, his arms weighed by piles of serviettes and Tupperware *plates with triangular partitions for measured portions. Œ swoons.*

Œ. *Tjitje dee Oarm* —

C/O glances up and accidentally drops her pen. She shudders and her elbow knocks the pocket diary from the table onto her lap.

Œ. Not now . . . Okay, look at the arms on *daut Mennoniet!*

Pause. C/O winks at Œ. Pause. Œ glowers. C/O gasps. Pause. Œ waves at the male orderly with a kerchief.

Œ. Woo-hoo. *Woo schient'et?*

> *A female attendant enters through the door and snaps a terrycloth bib.*

Œ. Keep your head down. Remember? Head down! You will choke yourself to death, Connie.

> *C/O rises from her chair, pulling on the polyester tablecloth, which exposes Œ's hamhock haunches. Œ straightens her hem. C/O masticates slowly and takes her seat again.*

Œ. *Joh*, you like my dress? I ordered it. *Simpson-Sears* ad. My poor, poor mailman dropped it off the week before last. Some little electronic trinket I did not ask for, yet too. Happy Mother's Day, I guess.

> *Œ absent-mindedly fans her hands on her lap and flattens the floral patterned crepe — crocuses? C/O gasps and grasps at her own throat.*

Œ. You can always hear him hoofing it. He shuffles — *ooda scheedle* — and slouches. With a crutch. On account of his hobbled foot. Never healed up proper. A war wound, you see. Crippled him.

> *C/O bends over, pulling the cloth off the table. Plastic plates collide with ceramic mugs, issuing their contents on the floor. Mayhem ensues. The female attendant rushes toward C/O.*

Œ. *Heimlich! Schnell!*

C/O. (*Coughs. She shakes her head, gazing at the male orderly.*) Danke schoen.

> *The male orderly grabs the female attendant by the shoulder, turning her. He grasps C/O to perform the manœuver. Her bust line jumps. He hefts her toward him over and over. C/O snarls syllables through clenched dentures at Œ.*

RECEIVED PRONUNCIATION IS THE FIRST CASUALTY OF A FORKFUL

To mouth sounds
To talk out of the other side
To shape air
To mould

Dummy those nouns
Total olfactory butter sign
Lush metaphor
Doom golem

Dung anærobic
Daunt bacteria udders brine
Larynx ærosol
Tumultuous

IN WHICH SHE CHEWED ON *RÜAK'WORSCHT* TO SPEW AN ŒSOPHAGEAL
UR-CANTO

ə a ə ō i
ä a i ē ä ə ī ə
a i e ə ō
ə ə ə ə

OR PORCINE *UR*-SONATA

        Dü aundra Oasch'loch
        Daunz dee Ve'füle enn'schwiene sindje
        Dee Täa sinje Vaspa Ope'mül
        Dee Launde'sproak

                                    brown
                                     well.
                                ms. Sauce
                               age is made.

                           Mrs. Katya Vogt
                              Winnipeg, MB

WRENNETJE

Dough:
  Sweet cream size of egg
  1/2 tsp. salt
  2 egg whites
  All-purpose flour for soft dough

Blend well. Roll out thin and cut into circles or squares.

Cheese Filling:
  Dry curd cottage cheese size of
    2 eggs
  1 tsp. salt
  yolks of eggs above

Combine all filling ingredients. Place a forkful onto dough circle or square. Fold into half-moon shape or triangle. Seal edges with fork. Drop into boiling water and boil for about 10 minutes. Pour on Schmaund'fat, and it is all gravy. Serve with fried farmer's sausage (with *Gnurpel*). While sprinkling cracked pepper, egg diners on by hinting that some vermin droppings must have fallen through perforated ceiling tiles onto the stovetop during preparation. Belly laugh, hearty and hale, at your own spott.

                    Mrs. Shepard Harold Hamm
                              Rat River, MB

SCHMAUND'FAT FOR WRENNETJE

Melt 3 to 5 tbsp. butter in small frying pan until slightly browned. Add 1 cup of heavy cream, stirring constantly, until gravy thickens. Season with drippings from fried farmer's sausage or *SPAM*. Mennonite manna!

                   Mrs. Doerksen-Dycksche,
                          mother in Israel

SUBSTITUTION

Replace butter with pig lard or rendered animal matter if desired. Or margarine. Or any edible oil product, to be honest.
Do not fry. No sauerkraut.

GLOMMS WRENNETJE

3 cups cottage ch
3 egg yolks
  pinch of em
  dash of p
Moral fibre

Mix well and

Take:
  1 cup milk
  3 egg whi
  1 tsp. s

  Enough
Roll out
mixture
press
form
min

CATASTROPHE: TWO WORDS

> SCENE 2. Œ throws a forkful of corn (dee Korn) at the male orderly. He turns away from the table he is wiping and moves toward the culprit. C/O flings links of fried farmer's sausage (dee Rüak'worscht) and a few perogies (dee Wrennetje) in cream gravy (dee Schmaund'fat) at the orderly. He oscillates to stare down Œ. Both women cross arms in defiance, stifling laughter. C/O gossips around the back of her liver-spotted hand.

C/O. Yesterday I saw the name on Mr. Postman's uniform. 'Roman Dyck'? It sounds as though his, you know, *tjlien Schwaunz*, his little tail, roams about, like I said.

Œ. *Oba joh*, Connie. *Daut's miene groote worscht*. Whole hog.

C/O. Words. (*Silence.*) Only two words.

Œ. What a name on him.

C/O. (*Coughs.*) Not only two words, though. That name is a sentence.

> Silence. Œ rummages through her parsimonious purse and offers C/O a lozenge.

C/O. Shepard did not even speak two words to me once he, well. (*Whispering.*) He turned.

Œ. Eli is his Christian name.

C/O. Can you repeat his name? I did not quite catch it. Eli? You mean, Korneelius? Dyck? No, not him.

> A pocket diary falls from C/O's lap onto carpet. She retrieves the booklet and a sheet of poesy flaps out. The letter is marked 'return to sender.'

>> By the time you read my admission it will be posthumous. So long I have suffered sin-

cerely without you son. The last scion.
Shepard Harold. Hal. Reading communiqués
you send from the front lines buoys my
spirit.

   Sin . . . cerely in . . . In sin . . .
I try to sign the letter sin . . . honestly
or truly, only my hand stops when I type
'Sin . . .' Each time, my knuckles spiral.
You'll have to settle. Seriously.

   I sinned against you when I was known
by another name. Harold Dyck. I changed
it for I couldn't bear the contempt of
field hands. They sung out 'Hairy Dick.'
I thought 'Fleeschmaun' had a ring to it.
I was raised a gentlemen farmer, high on
the hog. I was 'fleesch'foawijch,' after
all. I thought again. I could not get
used to the name 'Meat-man.' Not in a
pig's eye. 'Hamm' was more copacetic.

   I sinned against you when I took another
helpmeet, Ethel, and went back to my last
name. Then we had this whelp named Korne-
elius. Eli. I sinned again against you
when I became a gentile shepherd.

   A crook calls you, Hal. The rod and
staff comfort you. Come. This trigger
of a Remington 51 points the way home.

   Bury my typewriter. I beg you. Forgive
me. For giving you up. Give up.

   (As you already know, I'm drawing this up
under observation.)

   Godspeed,

OUR HUSBANDMAN

skins himself over the vanity. Pulls his corpuscles. Squints. Drags on straight razor. Rinses in standing water turned to resin. A coil of nerve endings chokes the drain. That is to say, you must not squander our husbandman's

    ink

       N
          /pyü·trəd/   /fēv·rish/   /bē·faəl/   /fil·thē/

      in
          /dē·trī·təs/   /drek/   /də·brē/   /e·pə·dərml/

    pin
          /nat/   /taŋ/   /nash/   /saŋ·gwən/   /ē·nig·mə/

    tine
          /strī·dant/   /trī·bəl/   /əl·y·lant/   /an·tē/

Our husbandman sinks pointer and thumb in a tepid pool. Plucks the plumbing root. Unnerved tendril recoils into pustules. Draws his razor across a strop turned to flypaper glue. Winces. Needless to say, that's not the way you were raised.

    Latinate   Germanic
        /a·gri·kəl·chūra/   /haůz·bȯnda/

CATASTROPHE: MALE ORDERLY

SCENE 3. A single round table remains in the middle of the cafeteria, with two elderly ladies bent over their partitioned Tupperware. *With a rheumy movement, Œ drops her fork on a calloused heel of bread and coughs. At the same time, C/O stifles a phthisic snigger.*

C/O. . . . no, not him.

The female attendant wheels an empty gurney through the cafeteria. Œ trains on the gurney.

Œ. (*Glaring into her souvenir mug.*) What is that? The smell of rat?

FEMALE ATTENDANT. Legion fever. Sewer backed up from the septic tank. It's because you old-timers insist on using pages from the *Sears* catalogue on the can.

C/O. (*Coughs.*) Shh . . . no.

Œ. (*Produces tissue from her sleeve.*) Gesundheit.

C/O. Oh! Of all things! Roman is Shep —

As the female attendant enters, C/O coughs. Pause. She swallows hard, spasms, and gurgles.

FEMALE ATTENDANT. Mayday, mayday! We have another one here.

C/O. Shepard is . . . oh. Brother. (*Whispering.*) Never.

Œ. (*Shaking her head.*) Bride at every wedding; corpse at every funeral; adult at every baptism.

The male orderly rushes in, sees C/O convulse, he mutters, and exits with the female attendant.

Aules haft en Enj; Bloß de Worscht haft twee Enja.

   & /
OR

   & orthodoxy dictates interment of a believer inside
       of three days /
or the deceased will not rise alongside Three-in-One

   & the departed will arise in dusty Sheol during the
       Judgement Day /
or Second Coming

   & it figures that immigrant Mennonites should build
       mausoleums into Manitoban loam of this Crown land /
or sepulchers to anchor their buoyant mortal remains

   & doctrine stipulates that cremation is a pagan sin /
or G-d would have offered the Son for a funeral pyre

   & after returning from war father became *een Prädja* /
or carpenter of the cellar where we weathered storms

   & vowing he must go in the grave whole father built
       a pine casket /
or a bespoke suit of lumber from a half acre of Hell

   & we sealed up seams in foraged boards with asphalt /
or he tacked up knots in stained planks with bitumen

   & to assure the pitch was seaworthy he rafted along
       the Rat River /
or to ensure the craft was comfy he napped all alone

   & while afloat he figured out the error of his ways /
or the grounds for why he must set his vessel ablaze

   & he wore dark robes to cut a limestone memorial to
       Christ's tomb /
or to cement his testimonial for that Son catacombed
       by Centurions

LEITMOTIF

In short, among many vagaries of the dossier, Nada clearly cannot shoulder the burden of proper description in his 'paper chase.' As a result, the Crown Corporation was forced to redact his error-ridden submission. Given the degree to which the stolen correspondence had mouldered into compost under Nada's watch, at this very moment of writing any attempt to salvage the black mulch for delivery would be wasted. Disinterred documents were measured in inches and weighed in pounds. The summary of contents of the smoldering post office follows: approx. 43 ft of lettermail, 89 ft of registered articles, 64 ft of unaddressed admail, and 43 lbs of parcelpost. These rough figures do not account for undeliverable mail, illegible, unintelligible, or incomprehensible mailable matter. Miscellaneous articles in Tpr. Dyck's barrows include a tool belt, ham radio, portable typewriter, food containers, and an electronic trinket (appears to be the little "Instant 'Trans-E-Later!'" of yours).

NATHAN DUECK lives in Calgary. His previous work, *king's(mère)* (2004), interprets William Lyon Mackenzie King's biography with prose poetry.